As the liners return to Liverpool's new cruise terminal, Great Mersey Liners is the first photographic panorama dedicated to the earlier golden era when the river rode on the crest of the waves that Britannia ruled.

With trade routes stretching across the world, Liverpool, by definition, was a world-class city. From Princes Landing Stage, by Liverpool's Pier Head, liners sailed for the Caribbean, Canada, India, the Far East, Madeira, Spain, Portugal, North and South America.

These liners' names still romantically resonate: Accra, Apapa, Aureol; Reina del Mar, Britannic, Mauretania, Sylvania, Carinthia, Voltaire and Van Dyck. Liverpool's imperial family were the white Empresses of Britain, England, Canada, France and Scotland.

So sit back and enjoy the memory of this exciting and glamorous era, thanks to the talent and dedication of the Liverpool Post & Echo's terrific photographers without whom this volume would not be possible.

Peter Elson, Liverpool Post & Echo

Above SIGNATURE SKYLINE: Anchor Line's M/V Caledonia lies off Princes Landing Stage and the Pier Head's world famous buildings in late summer, 1953

REGAL BIRTH: Arguably the most beautiful postwar liner built anywhere, RMS Windsor Castle, fussed over by a gaggle of Cock tugs,
leaves Cammell Laird's shipyard, Birkenhead, for her rudder to be fitted in Gladstone Drydock, Bootle, in May, 1960, prior to her sea trials and
maiden voyage on August 18, 1960, as flagship for Union-Castle Line's UK – South Africa express mail service. She was the company's last ocean
liner and was withdrawn in September, 1977

SMOKE TRAIL: Some 22 years before Windsor Castle's debut, more Cock tugs guide Cammell Laird's previous premier liner contract, Cunard Line's Mauretania (II). "The Maury" also moves down the Mersey to have her rudder fitted at Gladstone Drydock, on May 14, 1938

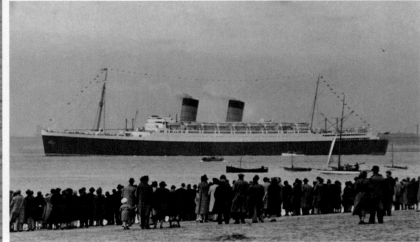

Top   Mauretania steams past Liverpool Docks on June 17, 1939, on her maiden voyage to New York, with Isle of Man steamer Mona's Queen inbound

Middle Mauretania swings around in the Mersey leaving Princes Landing Stage at the start of her maiden voyage

Above The maiden voyage is underway as Mauretania gathers speed in the Crosby Channel passing well-wishers on the tip of Wirral

CENTRE POINT: The strikingly flared bow of Blue Funnel Line's brand new M/V Centaur is graced with an attractive plaque of the mythological figure as she comes alongside Princes Landing Stage in January, 1964, after her shake-down cruise from the Clyde

HELLO GOODBYE: Built for £2m by John Brown & Co, Clydebank, this was Centaur's only visit to her home port, being specifically designed for passenger and sheep travel between Fremantle, Australia, and Singapore. The woolly ones possibly hastened her demise, allegedly their urine rotted her steel plates and she was withdrawn in November, 1982

IMPERIAL ARRIVAL: Excited crowds gather on Princes Landing Stage, Liverpool, as Canadian Pacific's brand new flagship Empress of Canada comes alongside to load passengers for her maiden voyage to Quebec and Montreal, on April 24, 1961

Top   SAINTLY LEAVE: Booth Line's great favourite SS Hilary departs from Princes Landing Stage on her first voyage to Manaus, 1,000 miles up the River Amazon, on August 15, 1931
Above FLAG DAY: Dressed overall, Canadian Pacific's Empress of England's derricks lift cargo aboard, on April 20, 1957, prior to her maiden trip to Quebec and Montreal

FANCY FLAGGING: A classic four-masted Bibby liner, either Oxfordshire or Yorkshire, left, prepares for a cruise, while St Tudno, of Liverpool & North Wales SS Co loads for Llandudno and Menai Bridge, on August 5, 1934

DUSKY LADY: After nearly a century Anchor Line's celebrated Glasgow – Mersey – Port Said – Suez – Aden – Karachi – India service closed, when Circassia made her last round voyage to Bombay. Here is the famously pristine 1937 motor liner moored at East Quay, in the Birkenhead twilight on January 14, 1966, prior to sailing almost full with 285 passengers and 4,000 tons of cargo

MASTER'S ORDERS: Capt Angus Colquhoun signals "Stop" on the Chadburn's bridge telegraph, after return to the Mersey at the end of Circassia's last Anchor Line 13,000 mile round voyage from Bombay, on March 15, 1966

PIPED MUSIC: Ex-Livepool Scotish piper Dave Renton, of Wallasey, plays his lament as Circassia docked at Princes Landing Stage for the last time on return from Bombay, on March 15, 1966, bringing most of her 300 passengers to the rails

CABIN SERVICE: Just before Circassia's last outbound voyage, on January 14, 1966, second steward Percy Sunter, of Speke, chats with passengers Mr and Mrs Harold Ryder, of Halewood, and their children John, four, and Katherine, who turned two on the voyage. Mr Ryder was a chartered engineer with English Electric, Netherton, and was seconded to an Indian company for two years

PICTURE PERFECT: Liverpool Photographic Society members record a busy scene overlooking Riverside Station and Princes Landing Stage with one of White Star Line's "Big Four" liners Adriatic, embarking passengers for a cruise, on August 5, 1931. Adriatic is surrounded by the Wallasey luggage boat, left, and Liverpool & North Wales SS Co's paddle steamer, St Elvies, far right; standing off is White Star's tender Magnetic with a Mersey Docks dredger at rear

GREAT LADY: Cunard Line's much eulogised four-funnelled RMS Aquitania gets steam up for Queenstown (now Cobh) and New York as a plethora of victuals and passengers arrive at Princes Landing Stage, in April, 1919. A luggage boat lies to the left

Top INTEGRATED TRANSPORT: The London boat train arrives at Liverpool Riverside Station, pre-First World War
Above SIDEWALK: Passengers disembarked directly from Riverside Station trains, walking across the fine glass-covered Princes Parade and onto their waiting ships

HEAVE HO: Two Alexandra Towing Co tugs belch smoke as they pivot Cunard Line's Ascania away from the pontoon, as she sets sail for Quebec and Montreal, watched by spectators aboard Elder Demspter Line's Apapa, about to leave for West Africa, on October 7, 1954

VOYAGE OVER: Gloomier days at Princes Landing Stage as Apapa completes her 177th voyage 14 years later on September 20, 1968, withdrawn because of spiralling operating costs

TWO GRACES: Cunard Line's Sylvania, left, disembarks passengers from New York, simultaneously with Canadian Pacific's Empress of England, from Quebec and Montreal. Everything on the Liverpool side in this wonderful June 5, 1964 view has disappeared, bar the Titanic Memorial, bottom left

BIDING TIME: A classic tall-stacked Alexandra steam tug, Hornby, left, and a fleetmate doze ahead of Elder Dempster Line's Apapa, taken from an Isle of Man Steam Packet ferry

CROW'S VIEW: The expansive sports deck of Shaw Savill Line's new flagship, Northern Star, at Princes Landing Stage after a shake-down cruise, on June 10, 1962. St Tudno lies astern. Northern Star was built for round-the-world emigrant UK – Australia – New Zealand voyages

Top   LIVER BOAT: Northern Star and her elder sister Southern Cross were revolutionary passenger ships with engines and funnel aft, creating what is now the cruise liner standard design

Above SHAPELY STERN: Northern Star's tall tapering funnel, fine sheer and subtly curving lines as seen from a Mersey ferry

BLAZE AWAY: Fire destroyed Canadian Pacific's Empress of Canada (II) in Gladstone Dock, on January 25, 1953, attributed to a dropped cigarette butt in a cabin

LAID OUT: A day later smoke still pours from the gutted Empress after she capsized from the hundreds of tons of water poured aboard. She had just come out of drydock after winter refit. Note her crushed funnels

LAME LADY: By February 17, 1954, the Empress's burned out hulk was exposed by lowering Gladstone Dock's level by 24ft to aid workmen preparing for her righting. This was achieved by welding a row of tripods to the hull so steel hawsers could pull her upright from across the dock

BACK UP: By March, 1954, the buckled and twisted Empress of Canada was almost righted, as seen here with the tripods and buoyancy tanks attached to her starboard side. Behind her is Empress of Australia, ex-De Grasse, hurriedly purchased from French Line, to honour hundreds of bookings made by Canadian Pacific passengers travelling to Queen Elizabeth II's Coronation

LAST RITES: Earlier, at daylight on January 26, 1953, on-lookers crowd to gaze at this dying ocean monarch

WHITE VISION: Empress of Canada glides towards Princes Landing Stage to embark passengers on September 2, 1966, with the Birkenhead Queensway Tunnel Vent, Wirral hills and North Wales mountains behind

HORSING AROUND: The elegant period gym aboard Furness Withy's dollar-earning luxurious Queen of Bermuda, with instructor John McDonald, of Liverpool, testing the trotting horse, in January, 1949

Top   SHOW CASE: Pre-maiden voyage open day aboard Mauretania with visitors admiring a promenade deck mural by Charles Pears, at Gladstone Dock, on June 15, 1939

Above MEN AT WORK: Finishing touches are put to Empress of England's first class drawing room, on April 17, 1957, prior to her maiden voyage from Liverpool to Canada

BAR NONE: Empress of England's tourist class cocktail bar is prepared by bar-keeper Michael Williams, of Speke, before the liner's maiden voyage, on April 17, 1957

Top   SNAZZY: The American soda fountain aboard Cunard's Sylvania, built in 1957
Above CLASSIC: The newly-installed first class cocktail bar after Empress of Canada's postwar refit in July, 1947

PREMIER DINING: The classically inspired, sumptuous, grand hotel-style first class restaurant aboard Liverpool's most famous liner, Cunard White Star's M/V Britannic, of 1930

STATELY COMFORT: The first class lounge on Cunard Line's new Carinthia, in June 1956. After passengers complained about the flashier décor of her elder sisters Saxonia and Ivernia, Carinthia inherited some of Aquitania's Edwardian furniture as seen here

SARDINE TIN: Boy pupils crammed into a dormitory aboard Devonia, operating a British India Line's educational cruise, settle down for the night. Teachers are attired in a black-tie visit before dinner, in March, 1965. Devonia was originally Bibby Line's troopship Devonshire

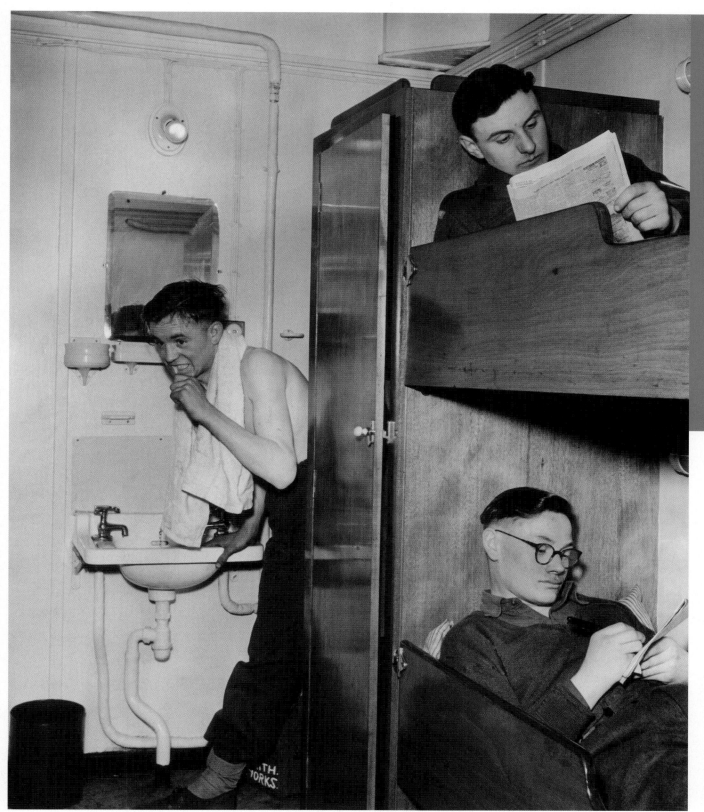

BUNKING OFF: The troopship Empire Clyde was equipped with cabins instead of dormitories and these three 19-year-old soldiers look marginally more comfortable than the school children as they prepare to leave Alfred Dock, Birkenhead, for the Far East, in January, 1955

LIVER BIRDS −2: All ashore after the last voyage of Elder Dempster's Apapa, on October 23, 1968, as stewardesses Lily Gooch, of Aintree, left, and Kay Tucker, of Lodge Lane, take bar keeper Harry Draper, of Gateacre, in hand

Top   TOOLING AROUND: Cunard liner Sylvania's store keeper Paddy Kelly, right, has just the pressure gauge for junior fourth engineer Norman Rowan, in March 1960

Above HOT METAL: The printer's shop aboard Sylvania, in May 1962, which daily turned out hundreds of menus, cards and The Ocean Times ship's newspaper

CHECKING IN: Crew members sign on aboard Canadian Pacific's Empress of France, all their working lives contained in discharge books heaped on the desk, seen on August 20, 1959

MR PASTRY: In August 1959, Empress of France's chief pastry cook Thomas Patten pipes jam into his tarts, just a few dozen of the 1,800 cakes he made each voyage

ENGLISH ROSE: Neatly uniformed stewardess Alice Lewis adjusts the first class flower arrangements aboard Empress of France

NET LOSS: One of Empress of France's officers oversees cargo discharge in Gladstone Dock, in August, 1959

EVENTIDE EMPRESS: Landing stage tugboat men ignore the stately presence of Empress of France as she steams down the Mersey on her first voyage to Canada after winter overhaul, in this atmospheric view of February 15, 1956

ALL SET: Canadian Pacific's brand new Duchess of Bedford is dressed overall for her maiden voyage from Liverpool to Canada, with CP's tender Bison alongside, on June 1, 1928. One of CP's most successful ships, she survived the war and lasted 32 years

NEW LOOK: After severe wartime losses, Canadian Pacific revamped Duchess of Bedford as Empress of France, seen here in Gladstone Dock, about to sail for Canada, in 1959. In her long career she carried 146,678 troops, 11,390 prisoners of war, 21,739 civilians and 86,249 tons of cargo

CHOCKS AWAY: The new 8,000-ton Hubert, of Booth Line, prepares for launching at Cammell Laird's shipyard, Birkenhead, on August 30, 1954. Hubert served on Booth Line's south Atlantic service from Liverpool to Brazil and the Amazon until 1964, when she became Malaysia, of Austasia Line, operating from Singapore

SITTING PRETTY: With anchors away during winter overhaul, Empress of France balances on her cradle in Gladstone Dock, in January, 1960, her last year of service

Top   FUNNEL AHOY: At Gladstone Dock, the floating crane Mammoth lifts off the aft funnel of Cunard Line's Mauretania during her massive
          postwar refit during September, 1946
Above NEARLY THERE: Freshly painted into peacetime livery, Mauretania has almost finished her refit by March, 1947, although the lifeboats are missing
          and deck awning frames for tropical wartime trooping still remain

LOST EMPRESS: Sold by Canadian Pacific to Shaw Savill Line to sail with its Southern Cross and Northern Star (see p26/27) to Australasia, Empress of England was extensively refitted at Cammell Laird, Birkenhead. Renamed Ocean Monarch, she leaves the Mersey on September 16, 1971

LOWER AWAY: Lifeboat drill takes place in Birkenhead docks aboard Bibby Line's Derbyshire, shortly before leaving for Rangoon, in January, 1961

STERN VIEW: After closing the New York run, Cunard Line's Sylvania restarted cruising from Liverpool in 1967 with a white hull for her new role. Here she undergoes winter overhaul, including a change of propellers. Note her stern anchor, de rigeur in case of being stopped in the narrow St Lawrence River

CRUNCH TIME: Caught by a sudden wind while moving in dock, Empress of England smashed against the lock knuckle and pinned the freighter Hindustan to the dockwall, on December 16, 1962

SUNSHINE SOVEREIGN: Furness Bermuda Line's magnificent Queen of Bermuda, of 1933, stalwart of the luxury New York – Hamilton, Bermuda service, rarely visited her Liverpool home port, but surely inspired the appearance of Cunard's much larger Queen Mary. She is seen at Belfast, in October, 1961, just before modernisation when her three funnels were replaced by a streamlined big single stack and a flared bow. Queen of Bermuda had already suffered the indignity of temporarily losing her third funnel during wartime to confuse the enemy over her identity. This made her the only liner to sail with one, two and three funnels

POOL BOYS: Well-dressed tile layers put the finishing touches to Queen of Bermuda's glamorous indoor pool after her postwar refit in January, 1949.
All very chic back then, including underwater pool lighting, hence her soubriquet of the "seagoing playground"

Top   REGAL FAREWELL: Now with single funnel and curvaceous bow, Queen of Bermuda is waved off to New York from Cammell Laird,
            Birkenhead after her annual refit in December, 1965
Above LOUNGING AROUND: Boasting nearly all first class accommodation for 731 passengers and few second class berths (for personal servants),
            Queen of Bermuda's plush interiors were in hotel de luxe art deco style, as in the lounge

MERSEY PANORAMA: It is a cold, sharp winter's day in January, 1957, but ships line Princes Landing Stage. From left are: Pacific Steam Navigation Co's flagship Reina Del Mar, on the eastern South America run; Elder Dempster Line's flagship Aureol, for West Africa; and finally an Isle of Man Steam Packet classic turbine steamer

FOND FAREWELL: The band strikes up alongside Liverpool's Lord Mayor, as well-wishers, families and friends pack Princes Landing Stage as Bibby Line's troopship Devonshire prepares to sail with the King's Regiment (Liverpool) for the Far East, on June 4, 1952

Top   SHIP SHAPE: Three years later in August, 1955, Bibby's Devonshire is considerably smartened up as she sails from Belfast for Singapore

Above HOME AGAIN: After landing from the troopship Empire Clyde, following three years tour of duty in Korea, the band lead the 1st Battalion, The King's Regiment (Liverpool) out of Princes Parade for a ceremonial march through the city, on March 1, 1955

FAR AWAY: A long way from her North Atlantic stamping ground, Cunard Line's Mauretania steams heartily through the Panama Canal on a wartime trooping voyage in April, 1940

BATTLE DRESS: Shaw Savill's former all-first class motor liner Dominion Monarch visits Liverpool while trooping during World War II.
She was replaced by the tourist class liner Northern Star (p26/27)

SCOTCH STOP: While the spotlight was on first class travel, emigrants to North America were shipping lines' real money-spinners. Empress of England gets underway for Canada from her Greenock anchorage, after being tendered by the Clyde paddle steamer Talisman, complete with piper playing Will Ye Nae Come Back Agin?

LEAVING LIVERPOOL: Sylvania wheels around from Prince Landing Stage, north Atlantic-bound, sometime in the early 1960s, with passengers crowding the upper decks, many of whom would be seeing their families for the last time

LIVERPOOL POOL: Plenty of crew members sign on for catering jobs aboard the liners at the Merchant Navy Pool in Paradise Street, with not much happening in the engine department

ENGINE

Top   BRUSHING UP: Painters refresh Mersey Docks & Harbour Board's green and cream livery on the ancillary
         buildings lining Princes Landing Stage during the 1950s
Above TERMINAL TRIP: The last train on Liverpool's Overhead Railway at Seaforth on December 30, 1956.
         The glowing tripod mast behind is Cunard's deluxe cruise liner Caronia, in Gladstone Dock

Top   SITTING TIGHT: Together for the first time, Canadian Pacific's Empress of France, England and
        Britain are strikebound in Gladstone Dock, in July, 1960
Above   UP THE CREEK: Rows over crewing levels led Cunard's new owners Trafalgar House to
        lay-up Franconia, front, and Carmania, in the River Fal, Cornwall, for a year until sale to
        Russia in August, 1973

STRIKE OFF: Organised chaos on September 11, 1960, at Princes Landing Stage as passengers board the famous Alexandra tug-tender Flying Breeze to reach Empress of England, anchored mid-river, right; meantime luggage is piled up to be loaded onto the Rea tug Langarth berthed head-on. Having mustered a full-crew, Cunard's Media, left, is ready to sail to New York

UNLUCKY LINER: One of Liverpool's most famous cruise liners was Cunard Line's Lancastria. Her life of sybaritic wanderings for the wealthy was cut short by the Second World War. Evacuating troops and civilians from St Nazaire after Dunkirk, she suffered a direct bomb hit on June 17, 1940, and more than 5,000 people aboard were killed, a story graphically told in Jonathan Fenby's book The Sinking of the Lancastria. Another Liverpool ship, John Holt, rescued hundreds of survivors from this catastrophe, Britain's worst Merchant Navy disaster ever

T.S.S. VANDYCK.

Top   OLD MASTER: During the desperation of the Depression, Lamport & Holt placed its liner Vandyck and sistership Voltaire on cruises
       from Liverpool and discovered untapped lucrative shiploads of passengers
Above RARE SIGHTING: Canadian Pacific's postwar trio for the first time together in Gladstone Dock preparing for winter cruises on November 27, 1963;
       beneath a Churchillian spectator are, from left, Empress of Britain, CP flagship Empress of Canada, and Empress of England

HOVER BOTHER: Smarting from the impact of jet travel, Cunard reintroduced its first postwar cruises from Liverpool, in April, 1967, with Sylvania, now with a tropical white hull. Seen in Valletta's Grand Harbour, Malta, on her second Mediterranean spring cruise, she carried a hovercraft seen here for tendering. This novel idea was not a success.

WATER PLAY: That this is a bit of a make-shift pool doesn't worry these girls on a school cruise aboard British India's Devonia, in the mid-1960s

Top FUNNEL FUN: Beneath the Cunarder Caronia's giant stack, cruise passengers enjoy deck games
Above DRY RUN: Finishing touches are put to Mauretania's indoor swimming pool at Birkenhead before her maiden voyage in June, 1939

OCEAN WAVE: These 11 teenagers are set for a 10-day schools' cruise to Bordeaux, Cadiz, Oporto and Tangiers aboard British India Steam Navigation Co's Devonia, seen just before the liner set off from Princes Landing Stage on October 11, 1967. Organised by Liverpool Education Authority, the cruise carried 802 pupils (paid for by their parents) from city schools, supervised by 50 local teachers

OUT OF BOUNDS
TO PASSENGERS

BOAT DRILL: A Devonia crew member checks the life jackets of Liverpool school pupils while aboard in 1964. Devonia was formerly Bibby's troopship Devonshire (see p69), made redundant when the Army switched to air transport

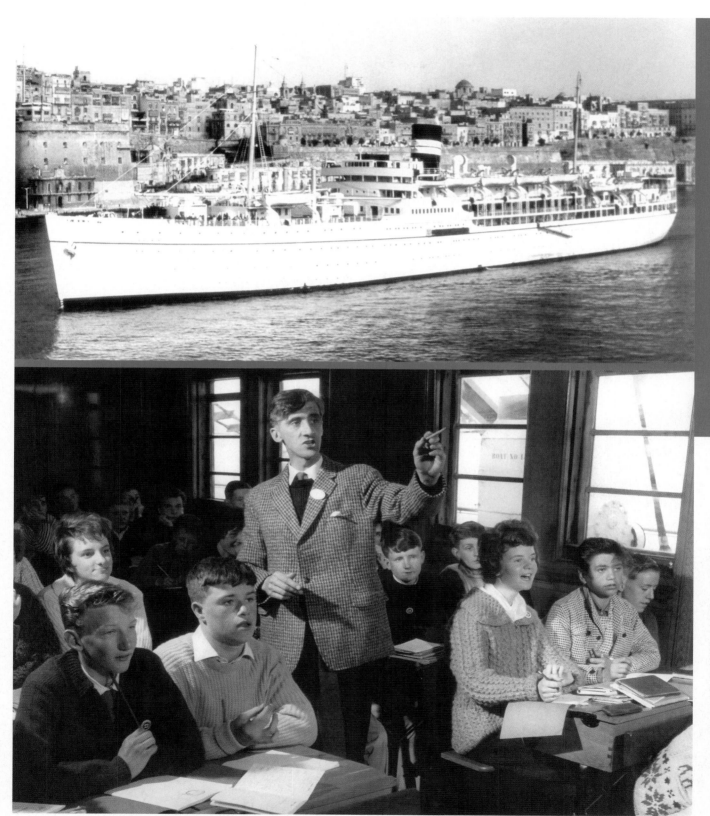

Top   SUN SPOT: British India's 12,800-ton Devonia at Grand Harbour, Valletta, Malta, on a cruise from Liverpool, in the 1960s
Above FLOATING IDEAS: A well-jacketed teacher and attentive pupils in a classroom aboard Devonia with the boat deck visible outside, in March 1964

QUEEN RETURNS: After an unfortunate grounding at Bermuda, the famous Mersey liner Reina Del Pacifo finally returns to Liverpool, in July 1957, squeezed into Gladstone Lock with the Alexandra tender Flying Breeze

Top   LOCKS GOOD: Pacific Steam Navigation's handsome Reina Del Mar, 20,263 tons, becomes the largest ship to use the new Langton Lock after returning from Chile, Panama, the Caribbean and Spain, in July, 1963

Above   BLUE FLUE: Blue Funnel's Dencalion, towed by a Rea tug, arrives at Birkenhead, in January, 1937. Dencalion was lost in Operation Pedestal, the Malta convoy of August, 1942

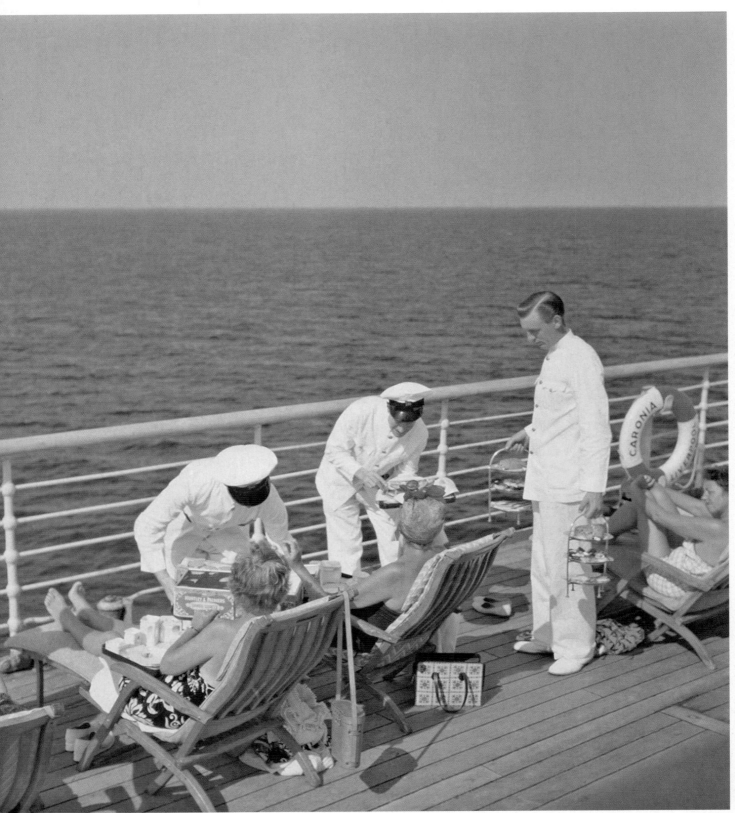

TEA-TIME: With a one-to-one crew-passenger ratio, these sunbathers are getting the ultimate afternoon service aboard Cunard's luxurious Caronia, dubbed the "Green Goddess"